Below Zero

Written by Claire Owen

Arctic

My name is Jocelyne. I live in the Arctic Circle. Can you think of some animals that live in very cold places? What do those animals do to help them survive over the winter?

Contents

Wherever you see me, you'll find activities to try and questions to answer.

The Arctic Summer

The central Arctic Ocean is covered with ice all year round. On the nearby land, snow and ice are present for most of the year. However, for about two months in the summer, it is warm enough for plants to grow. At this time of year, many animals of the Arctic are busy raising their young.

Arctic fox pups come out of the den when they are three or four weeks old.

A newly hatched snowy owl chick takes a rest.

Harp seal pups weigh about 24 pounds at birth. The pups drink milk from their mother and gain as much as 5 pounds a day. (You might gain 5 pounds in a year.)

Mother harp seals feed their pups for only 12 days! At the end of that time, how much would a pup weigh?

Dall sheep and kid

Siberia

Alaska

CANADA

ARCTIC OCEAN

North Pole

GREENLAND

ICELAND

Counting a Colony

Walruses like to hang out in large colonies of 1,000 or more. Walruses can grow 14 feet long and can weigh as much as 3,000 pounds, so 1,000 walruses take up a lot of space! Scientists count the walruses in a small area. Then they use that number to estimate the total number of walruses in the colony. This method is used for estimating other animal populations, too.

estimate   to make a general but careful guess

In the picture below, count 10 of the walruses. Then estimate the total number. How many walruses do you think are on the beach at the left?

Winter Approaches

When the days become shorter and colder, most animals migrate to warmer areas in the south. A few animals prepare to spend the winter in the Arctic. The female polar bear digs a den where she will sleep and give birth to her cubs.

migrate   to move from one area to another for feeding or breeding

The polar bear is the largest bear in the world. It is also the largest carnivorous land animal. A polar bear stands more than 8 feet tall.

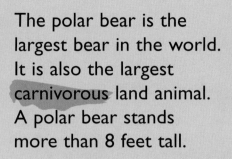

Choose a bear from the chart. How much heavier is the male than the female? Now pick two bears. What is the difference in body length?

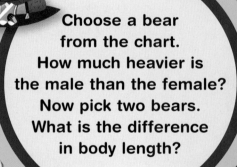

BEAR ESSENTIALS	Polar Bear	Brown Bear (Grizzly Bear)	Black Bear (American)
Body Length	100 in.	80 in.	75 in.
Weight (Male)	1,350 lb.	850 lb.	650 lb.
Weight (Female)	650 lb.	450 lb.	300 lb.

carnivore   an animal that eats mostly meat

Snowy Nomads

Snowy owls are the largest and toughest birds in the Arctic. Their wings can measure more than five feet across. Their plumage protects them so well that they can survive at minus 40 degrees Fahrenheit. Snowy owls prey on foxes and weasels and on other birds. They are fast and strong enough to knock a person to the ground!

Snowy owl eggs hatch every 2 days. In a clutch of 7 eggs, how old would the first chick be when the youngest chick hatches out?

Female snowy owls have a two-day break before laying another egg. Adult owls protect their chicks until they are about 9 weeks old, when they are able to fly and hunt on their own.

Did You Know?
The stiff feathers around the snowy owl's eyes reflect sound waves toward its ears.

plumage   the feathery covering of a bird

Snowy owls are the nomads of the north. Satellite tracking systems show that snowy owls fly across large areas of the Arctic after they have raised their young.

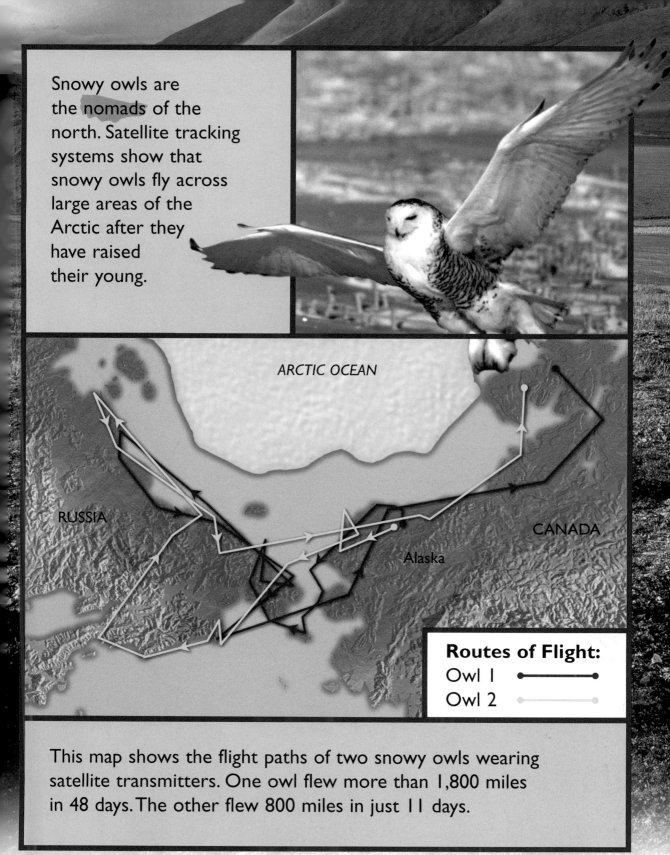

ARCTIC OCEAN

RUSSIA

CANADA

Alaska

Routes of Flight:
Owl 1 ●————————●
Owl 2 ○————————○

This map shows the flight paths of two snowy owls wearing satellite transmitters. One owl flew more than 1,800 miles in 48 days. The other flew 800 miles in just 11 days.

nomad   a wanderer, moving from place to place according to the food supply

Amazing Migration

The Arctic tern is a small bird about 13 inches long. It breeds in the Arctic during the summer. In the winter, the Arctic tern flies south to Antarctica. It returns to the Arctic the following year. This is the longest migration made by any animal in the world!

Use the Scale on a Map

Work in pairs to figure out how far the Arctic tern flies each year. You will need scissors, string, and a ruler.

1. Carefully place a piece of string along the Arctic tern's migration route (on page 13).	3. Use a ruler to measure the length of the string (in inches).
2. Cut the string to match the length of the migration route.	4. Use the scale to figure out the length of the route. (Each inch represents 1,000 miles.)

The Migration Route of the Arctic Tern

GREENLAND

NORTH AMERICA

SOUTH AMERICA

AFRICA

ANTARCTICA

Scale:
1 inch = 1,000 miles

On the Move

Many animals of the Arctic migrate. Caribou make the world's longest migration by land. Herds of up to half a million animals travel about 400 miles each way between their summer and winter pastures. Gray whales make the world's longest migration by sea. Each year, these huge mammals travel about 12,500 miles—from Alaska to Mexico and back.

Gray whales swim very close to the coast. This has made the whales easy to hunt, and they have come close to extinction twice. Since 1946, gray whales have been legally protected. Today, their population is more than 20,000.

extinct when a group of plants or animals has died out

Figure It Out

How would you solve these problems? You may use a calculator to help.

1. Gray whales swim at an average speed of 5 miles per hour. They swim for about 15 hours a day. About how far does a gray whale swim in one day?

2. From Alaska to Mexico is about 6,000 miles. How many days would it take a gray whale to swim that far?

3. The first gray whales leave Alaska in early December. When would they arrive in Mexico?

4. In January, about 30 whales swim past the Oregon coast every hour. How many whales would swim past in 15 hours?

Sample Answers

> Do some research on insects that migrate. Which insect makes the longest migration? About how far does the monarch butterfly migrate?

Page 5   84 pounds

Page 10   12 days

Page 12   about 24,000 miles

Page 15
1. 75 miles
2. 80 days
3. late February
4. 450 whales

Page 16   The desert locust makes the longest migration of any insect (2,800 miles). The monarch butterfly migrates up to 2,000 miles.

Index